My Media Coach

My Media Coach

Barbara Clopton

Camp & Gee Publishing
2014

First Printing: 2014

ISBN 978-0-9903224-1-2

Camp & Gee Publishing
Sacramento, California 95814

Ordering Information:
       To order, go to www.lulu.com/shop. Special discounts are available on quantity purchases by corporations, associations, educators, and others.

To Ted and Minnie.

Contents

Introduction

Cameras are a part of our everyday lives. Love them or hate them, they capture a lifetime of moments we ultimately watch on-screen. From smart phones and computers to televisions or even movie screens, we're bound to appear on one screen or another. Most of the time, we're on-camera for fun. But sometimes, by choice or request, we may find ourselves working in front of cameras. Playing in front of cameras is easy. Working in front of cameras is not.

We may not be professional on-air talent, but we share the same desires when working in front of cameras. We want to look great and perform without making mistakes. We want the audience to take note of what we say or do and persuade them into liking us. It's not impossible. On-air personalities do it every day. If you're going to work in front of cameras, you need the same type of studio training and image consultations on-air professionals receive. That's what this book is all about.

As a working broadcast television and webcast director, I know what works and what fails on TV. I've given lots of industry advice while directing novice on-air talent over the years and now I'm providing it to you.

"My Media Coach" is a style and television studio guide for anyone who works in front of cameras. Whether you're an aspiring entertainer, a professional making a webcast or televised appearance, or you just want to make better selfies, presentations or internet videos, this book is for you. By putting you at ease about working in front of cameras, you'll be more comfortable with your on-camera experience. As you gain more confidence, your on-screen appeal and credibility will increase and you'll achieve your ultimate goal: winning over the viewing audience.

You'll learn broadcast industry secrets and a little about television production itself; its components, terminology, psychological effects, and how to use it to your advantage. Though broadcast industry terms in *italics* are scattered throughout the pages, this isn't an overly technical book.

You'll also get advice on how to handle the dark side of media exposure, such as scandal and cyber bullying, and be informed of your rights when dealing with media outlets. In short, you'll have all the tools you need to succeed in this media driven world. So relax, smile. You'll be great.

Download the e-book edition onto your smartphone or mobile device or take this guide with you to your next appearance. Use its checklists to make the most of your photo shoot, televised appearance or webcast event.

Chapter 1
Your Success Start with You

What It Takes to Be Successful On-Screen Talent

You might ask, what exactly is 'on-screen talent'? In director's terms, when the cameras are pointed towards you and you appear on television, computer, or movie screens, you are considered to be on-screen talent. Successful on-screen talent have the ability to generate on-screen appeal. So whether you're acting or being yourself, it's important for you to generate some on-screen appeal.

What is on-screen appeal? It is the personality everyone loves. It's the energy that keeps the audience interested in you. If you ask talent agents what they're looking for when scouting new talent, they often say, "I'll know it when I see it." It is the 'it' factor, as in "she has 'it'". It is a star quality which can't be defined. You can't fake it or buy it. Successful on-air personalities are born with it, nurture it, and use it to its fullest. You need to develop the 'it' factor in you. Consider Case Study #1 when working on your on-screen appeal.

Case Study #1 - American Idol

American Idol is more than a reality television show. It's not just a search for the next big singing sensation. Its big business and America is the target market.

In broadcast industry terms, America is broken into five television markets: the East coast, the Midwest, the Pacific Southwest, the South, and urban markets (top twenty urban area cities in television ratings, i.e. New York, Los Angeles, Chicago, etc.) A successful

American Idol participant must appeal to the majority of viewers in each of these markets in hopes of winning. But before they have a chance of winning over the markets, they must win over the show's producers.

What the producers (and judges) are looking for is basically what the public wants; a great singer (can sing any song in any key upon demand) with a great recording voice. Women must be vivacious, bubbly, humble, easy to work with, and have a nice smile. Men must be warm, sincere and appeal to women ages 15-24. Producers are looking for sexy without raunchiness. And they do not want to work with a diva.

In summary, American Idol winners and notable runner ups all share these winning qualities:

- Truly talented in what they do (good singing voice and vocal ability)
- Easy to work with (follows direction, eager to learn and happily participates in promotional activities)
- Humble
- Sincere
- Personable
- Impressed producers and judges with the total package (good looks, talent and professionalism)
- Appeals to the studio and viewing audiences
- Appeals to and wins over at least 4 out of 5 target audience markets according to *Nielsen ratings*, a broadcast surveying firm.

These are the qualities of successful on-screen talent. These are the 'it' qualities you must develop within yourself to succeed in media.

Beating Public Speaking Anxiety
As we discuss bettering your on-screen persona (your public image), let's address the number one problem people experience when appearing in front of cameras. Nerves. Speaking in front of an audience makes most people nervous. Adding lights, cameras, microphones, and monitors seems to worsen matters for even the most experienced speakers. They don't call it 'stage fright' for nothing.

Anxiety can manifest in various ways. You begin to shake, your throat dries and tightens, and you hear your heart beating in your ears. These are called nervous body cues. The fear of "messing up" can cause you to forget your lines, lyrics, speaking points, dance steps, etc. University studies have shown that, in fact, you do lose some of your thinking capacity when dealing with these nervous body cues. This is a problem when working in front cameras because you need all the brain power you can get to perform well. You need to learn how to handle your nervous body cues. If public speaking is a problem for you, here are some tips which will definitely help.

Create a positive empowering dialogue in your mind. Positive thinking and visualization can lead to positive results. U.S. Olympic gold medalists from a multitude of sports have been using this technique for years. Reassure yourself with a positive internal dialogue. Visualize yourself giving an outstanding presentation or performance to a warm receptive audience. Visualize their positive reaction. Do it every day when you wake up, after you practice your performance, and right before going on-air. Remember, people want to see you succeed.

Join a public speaking group. Groups such as Toastmasters offer tips, practice and support in public speaking. Consult the internet or your local phone book for a chapter near you.

Practice controlled breathing exercises. Controlled breathing increases oxygen flow to the brain. This stimulates mental processes and reduces anxiety. A well oxygenated brain has better memory, concentration, and problem solving capabilities. One simple exercise is to breathe in through your nose while counting to five (silently in your head), then exhale through your mouth while counting to ten. Repeat this cycle about six times. Meditate. Use this time to clear away negative thoughts.

Keep your mind and body active. Crossword puzzles and brain games have been shown to improve concentration and even stave off senility. Physical activity promotes health. Boosting blood flow throughout your body promotes faster thinking, better digestion, stronger muscles and more. The better your mind and body feels, the better you'll look and perform on-camera. So exercise your brain and body regularly to improve all aspects of your life.

Eat nutritiously. Eat foods that nourish your brain and skin such as vegetables, fish, fruit, and whole grain foods. Drink water, around

9 to 13 cups a day. Not only will you think better, your skin will look better on camera. Don't overindulge in salty foods or alcohol prior to show time. These foods increase puffiness in your face. Consult your doctor or nutritionist for the right diet for you.

Get plenty of sleep. You want to be sharp to answer questions, follow cues, recite your lines, etc. So get six to eight hours of sleep every night. Sleep deprivation not only plays havoc on your thinking skills, it can cause under eye bags and dark circles under eyes which show up big time on-screen. Don't stay out late the night before an important appearance. You don't want your night activities showing on your face.

People Want to Hear Your Message

Believe it or not, people want to hear your message. They wouldn't be tuning in or viewing your post if they weren't interested in what you have to say. You wouldn't have been invited to make a presentation or cook or perform if people didn't want to see you. The public wants to be informed, entertained, or compelled into action. They care about what you have to say. So always give them your best. Take the time to take care of yourself. Look for ways to improve you. Practice and improve your craft. Be prepared. Have confidence in your talents, knowledge and skills and you'll have success in everything you do. And as a friend of mine, who directs a nightly news show says, "It's only TV." It's not brain surgery or as important as piloting a plane. It's only TV.

Chapter 2
Use Colors to Look Your Best on Camera

Make Color Work for You
To understand how different colors affect your on-screen persona and make them work for you, you must keep in mind these three things: (1) how colors are perceived by the camera or monitor (2) how the color looks against your skin tone and (3) the cultural or psychological impact various colors have on viewing audiences. If you understand and apply these three principles, you'll make better, more persuasive wardrobe and make-up choices.

Understanding Color on Digital Screens
Digital images are made from light and shadows. Color is used to enhance the picture. What you need to remember is this: cameras use light and color to produce a picture. The ultimate reflector of light is white. The absolute absorber of light is black. Since black and white are extremes on the color scale, you want to keep them to a minimum and choose camera friendly colors that fall in between. You want to choose colors from a rainbow's spectrum that are lightly or fully saturated with color, and limit colors that absorb light. You want to choose clothing that strikes a good balance of light and color.

Color as a Psychological Tool
Color is a very powerful psychological tool. Through psychophysics, the study of stimuli upon people's perception, there are many documented studies on how colors psychologically affect people. Studies

have shown that changing a food packaging's color can stimulate sales or cause them to fall. Painting prison cells pink decreased inmate disturbances. A change of color from gray to yellow on a factory wall increased workers' productivity. Colors are also used to increase an object's visibility such as orange traffic cones. These are the testaments to the power of color.

In the field of industrial psychology, there is a sub-field dedicated to the psychology of color. Marketing professionals rely upon color research to get you to buy and remember their products. It's not from a lack of creativity that Coca Cola has used the same colors on their labels for over 100 years. When I mentioned Coca Cola, did the colors red and white come to mind? That's the power of color and packaging. Think of your wardrobe as your packaging.

How to Use Colors to Look Your Best on Camera

The following colors are the best colors to wear on-camera. Since you are more than likely to be *shot* (photographed and seen) predominately from the waist up, the emphasis of color relates to upper body clothing.

Best Colors

Pastels: light blues, pinks, lavender, light green and pale yellow. The camera loves pastels. Because they're lightly saturated in color, pastels bounce light up under your face, diminishing lines and wrinkles for a more youthful appearance.

The camera also likes darker shades of pastels: sage, dove grey, sky blue, peach, mauve and goldenrod.

Bright colors: orange, canary yellow, chartreuse, hot pink, and coral. Cool colors: aqua, teal, violet, turquoise, and periwinkle.

The camera also likes richly saturated "vegetable dye" colors: eggplant, pumpkin, mustard, and avocado; and dark neutrals like tobacco, charcoal grey, chocolate brown, and navy blue.

Color Cautions

The following pages contain a list of colors you should be careful of when choosing what to wear on-camera. They are most troublesome for cameras and/or certain skin tones to handle. Topping the caution color list are red, white and black.

Red

Red is not a camera friendly color. Monitors enhance color which makes red extra intense. Tomato and fire engine reds can *smear* or *bloom,* an unflattering effect where the color spreads outside the subject's original outline. This can make a person look larger than they really are. Although advanced digital cameras and HDTV (high definition television) produce crisp pictures in which smears have nearly been eliminated, smears and blooms still occur on older model televisions, monitors and second generation videotapes (videotape copies made from a copy.)

Psychologically, red is a commanding yet confrontational color. University studies have shown that red can change a viewer's mood. Researchers recorded increased tension and blood pressure within test subjects who stared at the color red for a period of time. Their studies determined that red conveys nervous energy.

On camera, red (and deep salmon pink) can accentuate redness in people with fair complexions or those who blush or sunburn easily. It may bring out an unflattering ruddiness in people with tanned skin. Red can accentuate acne blemishes and Rosacea, a skin condition where blood vessels close to the skin's surface cause a redness in the cheeks. If you fall into any of these categories, you may not want to wear a red shirt or jacket on camera.

A good alternative to red is orange. Orange is a camera friendly color that translates positively in cultures throughout the world. Because every TV set's colors are calibrated per its owner's personal taste, some tones of orange look red on-screen. From pumpkin to light apricot, orange suits every skin tone.

In summary, treat red as an accent color and wear it sparingly. Avoid bright red (fire engine and tomato red) shirts and jackets. If you must wear red, like a company shirt, then do so. Promoting your company overrides your need to look great. If you like wearing red, choose darker shades of red such as garnet or blood red.

White

White clothing, such as an all-white suit, presents problems only an experienced technical director or photographer can correct. Because white is devoid of color, it reflects all light. The camera's iris and/or studio lights must be turned down to prevent overexposure or a picture that is so bright that all definition is lost in glaring whiteness.

Camera settings and light levels are made well in advance, not live on air. If you walk on set last minute dressed in an all-white suit or you wear a white shirt under a dark jacket and take off the jacket seconds before going on-air, you're asking for trouble because light levels, which were set high to light a dim studio, must now be quickly adjusted to lower levels to accommodate your now bright shirt or white suit. If the production crew is inexperienced or doesn't care, these adjustments might not be made. For people with very fair or dark complexions, this can be especially problematic.

If light levels are set high, all-white outfits will overwhelm people with fair complexions. It removes color from fair faces especially if shot in front of a grey or beige background. Over-exposure can cause a "polar bear in a snow storm" effect where all you see are the subject's eyes. The subject's nose and other facial details can be lost in the brightness.

People with dark complexions absorb light. To compensate, either more physical light must shine on the subject or the camera's iris must be opened. Most camera operators will open the camera's iris as lights are already positioned and set to their maximum limit. Either way, these adjustments can't be done if the subject is wearing all white. As the camera receives more light, the white becomes brighter. This can make a dark skin tone even darker. It can be corrected in photographs or high budget movie productions but not during live television shows.

Good alternatives to white are pale pastels. Because they're lightly saturated with color, they're less bright than white but still looks crisp and light. Another good alternative to white are off-white colors, like cream and ivory.

In summary, wear white sparingly, i.e. a white shirt under a jacket, keeping the jacket on. Avoid white jackets and suits unless it's part of your uniform, i.e. a doctor's lab coat.

Black

As stated earlier, black is devoid of color. It absorbs all light. Black is a problem because we need light to make a picture.

Many people like to wear black pants and suits because they're slimming. That works on-screen if you combine it with some color (a colorful shirt, tie, or accessories.) It becomes problematic when you wear too much black.

Since black absorbs light, it's not the ideal color for people with dark complexions. If you have a dark complexion, wearing all black will make you look even darker. This can be corrected in photographs but when you're shooting a TV show and the lights aren't bright enough or the camera operator doesn't make adjustments to the camera (opening the iris for more light), you run the risk of looking like a dark, shapeless blob. If you're not appearing on a controlled network television or film set or you're shooting your own home videos, these adjustments are not likely to be made.

If you have fair skin, wearing too much black will drain color from your face. Also people with fair skin who dress in head to toe black and shoot in front of an all-black background run the risk of creating the 'floating head' affect, where all you see is an animated head and hands devoid of a body floating in the darkness.

When wearing all black, the clothing's definition, its shape, layers, trim, tailoring or embellishments can be lost in blackness. Choose black clothing that exposes skin such as a short sleeve V-neck shirt, a sleeveless little black dress or clothing with cutaways in the fabric. If you dress in all black clothing, wear different finishes of black i.e. a black silk shirt under a matte black wool jacket with a black satin tie or black velvet vest.

Psychologically, black clothing can make you appear mysterious or sinister. Mysterious might be good for a singer or actress but I wouldn't wear a black shirt under a black pinstripe suit if I was a defendant in court.

In summary, avoid dressing all in black. Obviously, this doesn't apply to religious or mourning attire. If you wear a black suit, add some color. Wear a colorful shirt, tie or blouse underneath. If you wear a black shirt or turtleneck, pair it with a colored jacket. If you really want to dress in all black, make sure you are shot against a colorful background i.e. red carpet event and not a background of black. Great alternatives to black are navy blue, charcoal grey and chocolate brown.

Blue

The camera likes the entire spectrum of blue. However, light blue clothing can interfere with *blue screen* technology, a blue background special effects screen used in movie and television productions. You see blue screen used on your local news, typically during the weather segment, where the weather man stands beside your local map and points to moving weather patterns. If the weatherman wore a baby blue turtleneck and pants, his body would disappear into the map while his head and hands float in space. Blue screen isn't used in simple interviews but may be used in remote interviews. Keep that in mind when making your wardrobe selection. Watch the show on which you'll appear to see if blue screen is being used for your segment or ask the producer or studio contact. Blue screen also comes in green which is fast becoming the industry standard.

In summary, blue is a good color choice for everyone but don't wear robin's egg blue clothing or clothes with light blue patterns if you're appearing in front of blue screen technology.

Green

Although most greens look good on television, people with pale blonde hair should avoid lighter hues of green. Green sometimes lends a green tint to blondes which can make their hair look light green on-air.

Also, blue screen technology comes in green (*green screen.*) The same effect that occurs in blue screen will happen when wearing green in front of a green screen. Again you most likely won't be appearing in front of green screen. Just be aware.

Natural, Neutrals, and Flesh Tones

Although neutrals are good alternatives to white and black, beware of neutral colors (oatmeal, wheat, beige and khaki.) These non-colors lend no color to your skin tone and can actually drain color from people with fair skin tones, especially if you're shot in front of a beige or grey background. You may blend into the wall. The same goes for flesh tones such as cameo pink. They lend no color to skin tones and tend to wash out under bright lights. Darker toned neutrals with deeper saturation, such as taupe, mauve and putty are better choices.

If you wear neutrals, accent them with a bright accessory like a red tie, coral jewelry, red lipstick, gold shoes, a pink evening bag, etc. In summary, avoid neutrals that closely match your skin tone. Avoid neutrals that blend in with the set's background. Wear them sparingly or with color.

Grey

Grey isn't the best or worst color for a camera lens to handle, but there are some cultural interpretations you should keep in mind. Grey conveys a sense of stability and trustworthiness but it can also be interpreted as old and stodgy. Its effectiveness depends on the wearer's age, the intended audience's age, and the shade of grey worn.

People under the age of 40 should not wear light grey suits. In a study of corporate hiring, interviewees in their twenties who wore light grey suits lost out to their counterparts in black, navy, and charcoal grey suits. Light grey is the opposite of a 'power suit', especially for the young. Light grey is a color which works best on older, established people.

When choosing to wear grey, the darker the grey, the better. Charcoal grey should be kept in mind because it's a great alternative to black and is in the power suit category. (Read about power suits in the Suits section on page 25.)

Matching the Right Colors to Your Skin Tone

Finding the right color for you depends primarily on your hair color and skin tone. Your hair is your face's frame and is a good indicator of which color grouping works best with your skin tone. Here is an easy guide for picking the best colors for you. They are based on your natural hair color.

Brunette – Your best colors are neutrals, pastels, brights, cools, and vegetable dyes. Avoid crowding dark clothing (particularly black) around your face i.e. a black turtleneck.

Blonde – Your best colors are pastels, brights, cools, and black. Keep red and green to a minimum as red can sometimes bring out redness in your skin tone and some greens can lend a green tint to your hair on camera.

Black – Your best colors are vegetable dyes, pastels, neutrals, brights and cools. High contrast neutrals of black and white should be kept to a minimum.

Redheads – Your best colors are neutrals, pastels, cools and vegetable dyes. You can wear bright colors but keep in mind that bright colors will accentuate the redness of your hair.

If your hair is dyed another color than your natural hair color, you may consider less saturated colors from the dyed hair's color group. People with grey, white or salt & pepper hair or are now bald should stay within their natural hair color category.

Director's Tip

Watch the show on which you'll appear. Note the color of the show's set and coordinate your color choices to the set's colors. You should wear contrast or compliment colors in relation to the set's color. For example, if the set is blue, your wardrobe should include contrast colors such as orange, shades of orange (peach, coral) or compliment colors like light green, purple or lavender. Use the contrast and compliment color groupings below to coordinate your wardrobe to a set or outdoor setting.

Red - contrast color, green; compliment colors: purple and orange.

Orange - contrast color, blue; compliment colors: red and yellow.

Yellow - contrast color, purple; compliment colors: green and orange.

Green - contrast color, red; compliment colors: yellow and blue.

Blue - contrast color, orange; compliment colors: green and purple.

Purple - contrast color, yellow; compliment colors: blue and red.

Summary
- Wear camera friendly colors that flatter your skin tone
- Wear red, white, and black sparingly
- Wear colors you feel comfortable wearing, but don't be afraid to break out of your comfort zone and try colors which you don't necessarily love but flatter you on camera
- Wear colors affiliated with your company, organization or product.

Chapter 3
Making Your Wardrobe Choice

Introduction

As mentioned in chapter two, your clothing is your packaging. It's one of the most important elements you must keep in mind when planning an on-screen appearance. Choosing the right clothes to wear on TV is a nerve wracking experience. That's why professional stylists make good money telling people what to wear. But most of us can't afford a stylist. So what should we wear?

The first thing I tell people is that your clothing doesn't have to be expensive to look good on television. Costume designers turn inexpensive fabrics like cotton and polyester blends into expensive looking garments all the time. The second piece of advice is to make sure your clothing fits well and isn't clingy, constrictive, or made of thin material. And third, when making your wardrobe choice, choose breathable, wrinkle resistant clothing.

Best to Worst Fabrics

Cotton, cotton blends, polyester and light wool blends are all fabrics that work well on TV. Though cotton wrinkles, it's breathable and comfortable to wear for long periods of time. Polyester (rayon) is good because it's wrinkle resistant. Lightweight wool gabardine is good for suits and jackets because it's wrinkle resistant and drapes over the body's curves without clinging. I highly recommend clothing made of medium weight cotton, cotton blends, polyester or polyester blends, and wool gabardine to keep you cool, comfortable and wrinkle free. Make sure your cotton garments are ironed because wrinkles and creases are highly noticeable on camera.

Silk is a light weight material that feels great and photographs well, but perspiration can easily show up as dark marks and are almost guaranteed to appear during hot outdoor shoots. Also, silk is prone to static electricity which causes it to noticeably cling to your body's curves.

Satin is a smooth, clingy material which shows bulges. Unless you have a super rock hard body, avoid wearing something like a full length satin gown. Satin is not a breathable material. It can cause the body to perspire and just like silk, you will have noticeable sweat marks. Satin is also prone to static electricity. Satin should be worn in small amounts such as in men's ties or a woman's sleeveless top. Because it's a reflective material, it can appear cheap under direct sunlight and should be shot under studio lights. Satin should be reserved for costumes and special occasion dresses (prom, wedding, and bridesmaid dresses.)

Linen is cool and comfortable but wrinkles easily. Its deep wrinkles and creases are highly visible on TV. Avoid light colored (white, cream) linen shirts and jackets or if you wear them, make sure they're ironed and wrinkle free. You may want to remain standing when wearing linen. Wrinkles in linen are less noticeable in darker colors such as chocolate brown, moss green, or black.

Leather and suede are non-breathable materials. You may heat up under their weight. If you wear a leather jacket, wear it over a sleeveless shirt or light-weight T-shirt. An alternative to leather is manmade leather. Fake leather is light weight, less expensive than real leather and looks like real leather on-screen. The same goes for suede. Microfiber looks the same as suede on TV but weighs less making it easier to wear for long periods of time. Another issue with leather is that when it rubs against leather furniture, it can squeak and emit other embarrassing sounds.

Clothing with metallic finishes (i.e. sharkskin and lamé), metallic threads, rhinestones, crystals or sequins should be worn in small amounts, like sleeveless tops, ties, skirts or shoes. These reflective materials can cause glare or *flares* (unintentional spots of reflected light) in the camera's lens. These finishes should be used in costumes or reserved for special occasions (i.e. red carpet gowns.) Metallic finishes look best in muted neutral colors such as cameo pink, pewter, champagne, etc. And be warned, these metallic finishes never look the same under the studio lights as they do under store lights.

Beware of nylon and other sheer materials where the skin can be seen through mesh. They may look great under store or home lights, but sheer material becomes even more transparent under bright lights. The same applies to lace. Lace photographs well as long as there's a contrast between skin and lace, but lace becomes even more revealing under strong studio lights. You will see every seam and undergarment. If you want to wear lace on-air choose lace clothing that has flesh colored lining underneath to offset transparency. Tops or bodices made of lace are just as effective as a whole lace dress. Wear lace and mesh material in small amounts such as insets on tops or dresses.

Avoid shiny, clingy material like Spandex. This material looks cheap and tacky on-screen. It should only be worn in athletic gear i.e. gymnast or track and field uniforms or in theatrical costumes.

Avoid velvet and velour. Though they look good on camera, these are heavy, non-breathable materials that can retain deep creases. They should be reserved for winter festivities and children's holiday clothing.

Clothing
Shirts
Since you'll be primarily shot from the waist up, your shirt may be your most important piece of clothing. When choosing a shirt or blouse, you should choose something cool, comfortable, and can support a clip-on microphone. Stiff cotton button down shirts, knit Polo shirts, scoop neck and V-neck collars are best. Avoid high collar T-shirts, high neck turtlenecks, and shirts that slouch. These tops don't easily accommodate a clip-on microphone.

Stick with solid colored shirts. There are issues with patterned clothing which you'll read about in the 'Patterns' section.
Dresses
Always choose a dress that's appropriate for the show. The only concern about dresses is if they're too revealing (too short, tight, transparent, etc.) it can embarrass you with a malfunction or make you look trashy. Be careful wearing dresses that are designed to em-

phasize or expose a particular body part. Mini-dresses are great when standing but once seated, it rides up and exposes much more than you expected. High rise slits in designer gowns look great when you stand in front of a mirror but when you stride across the stage, the dress will open and expose more than you planned. Test out the dress in front of a mirror; stretch, reach, sit down, and hop. Make sure your dress securely covers your body. We don't want to offend the viewers and censors.

Jeans

In this increasingly casual world, it's acceptable to wear jeans to almost any event. Since the camera will more than likely be shooting you from the waist up, your jeans may not be seen. In any case, make sure your jeans are clean and unwrinkled. Wear a suit jacket or pretty blouse with your jeans for a more professional, upscale appearance.

Undergarments

Unless your underwear or lingerie is intended to show, your underwear should not be noticeable. Wear flesh-colored undergarments that match your skin tone or black lingerie. We don't want to see a white bra strap fall from underneath your sleeveless top or hot pink panties under your white pants.

Also, if you are wearing form fitting clothes, you may want to wear shape-wear or body shapers, underwear designed to slim. I hate to say it but it's true, the camera does add weight to the body (around ten pounds.) Even if you aren't overweight, if you're wearing body hugging clothing, you may consider wearing shape-wear to avoid panty lines, help cinch in the stomach or smooth out any little bulges. Body shapers come in a variety of styles to suit all body issues; waist cinchers, camisoles and tanks, and thigh slimmers. They cinch in tummies, erase back fat rolls, and smooth cellulite off of thighs and buttocks. Keep in mind that you might be wearing it all day so choose lightweight, comfortable shape wear that allows you to breathe.

Suits

Suits add to your professional persona. They look good on-camera. Flattering in their structure, they enhance your credibility and define you as a professional. Suits are as individual as the wearer. A suit's combination of shirt, suit and tie can convey power, authority, maturity or humor. It can close a sale or make someone laugh. It's your choice.

Choosing the right suit is easy. You should wear a properly fitting suit that gets your point across to your target audience. Remember, your goal is to win over people. A suit usually helps. Here are some examples of suit combinations popular in many industrialized nations. They are listed from best to worst is terms of power of persuasion.

Power suits are well-tailored black or charcoal suits (with or without low contrast pinstripes) worn by executives. The term 'power suit' was coined in the 1980's when it became the uniform of highly successful Wall Street executives. They exude power which gives the wearer a psychological advantage over their peers. The suit is paired with a white button down shirt and solid colored tie. Add a silk pocket square and the power suit turns into an upscale business evening look.

Another popular look is a 'political conservative' look which is comprised of a conservative colored suit, dark grey to navy blue, with a white or blue button down shirt and red, blue or yellow tie. Typically the tie's color is the color of the wearer's political party though current trends find most politicians favor red because the color conveys energy.

A popular look among fashionable men is a 'monotone' look which incorporates different hues of the same color throughout the clothing. The best colors are masculine colors like dark grey, dark blues, black, and burgundy. The look also lengthens the body causing the wearer to appear taller.

A sports jacket is a good alternative to a suit jacket. It's structured, so you won't look slouchy, but casual enough to wear with jeans. Sports jackets are the traditional jacket of sports casters and college professors. They make the wearer seem more approachable. Focus groups have found that sport jacket wearers are viewed as trustworthy.

For women, power suits are good but if you want an alternative to a boys' club suit, you can wear pastel or colored suits. They're flattering without giving up the structure and authority of a suit. Many women tend to wear black suits because of their slimming qualities. If you wear a dark suit, wear a bright or light colored blouse underneath to lend color and bounce light up to your face.

Then there are ineffectual suits. These suits lend no power to your appearance and may actually work against you. Light colored suits (light grey, beige, cream) are the opposite of power suits. Only established professionals should wear these suits. They aren't recommended for people under the age of 40. Avoid colorless suits.

On the other end of the spectrum are vibrantly colored suits. Vibrant suits such as red, electric blue and mustard yellow are acceptable in some regions of the U.S. and the entertainment field but are not recommended for business as vibrant colors convey nervous energy. Also, some men feel confident enough in their manhood to wear pastel suits and can wear them with flair but keep in mind that pastel colors can lend an air of whimsy or femininity to even the manliest man.

Avoid wearing patterned suits (herringbone, hounds tooth, or high contrast pinstripes.) They can cause problems for the camera as described in the 'Patterns' section.

Sweaters

Though we're more comfortable in our favorite cozy sweater, they aren't the most flattering garments on-screen. Large cable knit wool sweaters add bulk especially around the mid-section and shoulders. Tight gauge knit sweaters hug all body curves. They have no structure and will make you look dumpy. Always choose to wear a jacket instead of a sweater.

Accessories

We use accessories like jewelry, shoes, and sunglasses to accentuate our wardrobe. They're great ways to express ourselves, but they can present problems during a television shoot.

Hats

Don't wear a hat. Obviously this doesn't apply to yarmulkes, Islamic kufis, hijabs, or other traditional religious head dress. Since studio lighting or sun light is overhead and shines down upon you, brimmed hats will cast an unflattering shadow over your eyes. This is especially true for baseball and cowboy hats. To cut the risk of unwanted shadows, tilt up the visor and set the hat back on you skull (though cowboy hat run the risk of tipping off the back of her head.) Baseball hats work better when worn backwards. Short brim hats (porkpie) are better than wide brimmed hats. Best advice, don't wear a hat.

Jewelry

Unless you are an entertainer, reality show housewife or promoting your jewelry line, keep jewelry to a respectable minimum. Jewelry can distract people from your message.

Necklaces, especially large chunky stone ones, can hit a clipped on microphone and cause unwanted noise. Jewelry that jingles, like charm bracelets or stacked bangles, can be a problem to audio. Large pieces of flashy jewelry made of diamonds or crystals can cast glare into camera lenses. If you wear large pieces of jewelry, like chandelier earrings, and they become a problem, be prepared to take them off and replace it with other jewelry you've brought.

Eyeglasses

If you can function without prescription glasses, do so. Eyeglass lenses can reflect studio lights or cast glare into the camera lens. If you can't see without them, by all means keep them on. You can alleviate glare by tilting the glasses a little lower on your nose. You may want to invest in contact lenses or an anti-glare coating on your eyeglass lenses.

Sunglasses

Don't wear sunglasses. The audience wants to see your eyes. People who wear sunglasses can be perceived as hiding something such as lying eyes or drug use. Sunglasses should only be worn by the seeing impaired and those with medical conditions where bright lights negatively affects their eyes. If sunglasses are part of your act then wear them. If you really need them because you're shooting outdoors in bright sunlight, keep your sunglasses on prior to shoot and remove them immediately before going on camera.

Ties

Dress codes are much more relaxed than ever before but ties are still a part of corporate business attire. When choosing a tie, you should avoid patterns with small, high contrast close set dots, stripes, or patterns. A solid colored tie or one with wide diagonal stripes is a better choice.

Patterns

Most patterns are not camera friendly and should be avoided. High contrast patterns such as black and white stripes, polka dots, checks, herringbone, and hounds tooth are particularly problematic. They often cause a *moiré* effect, (a.k.a noise) where contrasting colors strobe into a vibrating rainbow because the camera is unable to keep up with rapid contrast changes between black and white. Close set patterns on moving clothing will strobe and moiré. The effect is very distracting to the viewer. Look for the moiré effect the next time you see a striped Oxford shirt on-air as they are some of the worst offenders.

Another group of troublesome patterns are animal prints like zebra, cheetah, leopard, Dalmatian, and snakeskin. In the wild, these patterns help an animal confuse its hunter or prey as it runs. They do the same to camera lenses. High contrast or close set animal prints like zebra, cheetah, snakeskin and Dalmatian spots are the worst for cameras to handle. Bold, low contrast animal prints like giraffe and tiger prints are the least troublesome. If you like wearing animal prints, where them as accents. Instead of wearing a cheetah print dress, you should wear a sleeveless cheetah print top under a jacket.

If you really want to wear patterns, choose bold, wide set prints. For example, if you wear something floral, choose a floral pattern which has large abstract flowers as opposed to small, high contrast close-set flower clusters.

Avoiding Problems with Patterns

As stated before, high contrast close set stripes and polka dots are not camera friendly. If you wear these patterns, use the following tips. There are no guarantees these tips will keep noise from happening because variables such as movement and camera distance come into play but your understanding of the problems will minimize the risk.

Shirts

Because shirts tend to be made of light-weight materials, they shift, slouch and drape against the body when the body moves. This movement causes diagonal stripes to moiré.

Don't wear striped Oxford shirts. They're guaranteed to moiré.

Avoid close set stripes with more than 12 alternating stripes per square inch.

Ties

Avoid close set vertical and diagonal stripes with more than 12 alternating stripes per square inch. Wear striped ties with large diagonal stripes of color where each stripe is at least a half inch in width.

Avoid small, close set polka dots. Polka dots should be spaced approximately one-quarter inch or more apart. This advice applies to shirts and dresses as well.

Suits

Typically, pinstripe suits won't moiré as long as the stripes are thin, low contrast stripes that are set wide apart. Pinstripe suits made of stiff materials like wool or polyester won't moiré. Light weight suits made out of seersucker will.

Windowpane patterns are okay if contrasting stripes are thin and/or set wide apart. This rule goes for shirts as well.

My advice, avoid patterns altogether. They may distract the viewer from your message. Don't risk it. Wear solid colored shirts, dresses, and jackets.

Stylists' Tip #1

Make sure your shirts and jackets fit properly. The camera will show any pulling and puckering of material. A good test to ensure proper fit is to put on the jacket, button the top buttons, and sit down. You should be able to comfortably slide two fingers between the jacket and shirt. If you can't, your garment is too tight and won't look good on-air.

Stylists' Tip #2

Stylists to the stars photograph their clients trying on potential red carpet dresses under bright lights. This way they can see how the color is interpreted by the camera and how sheer the garment looks on TV. You can do the same at home with a camcorder or camera. Photograph yourself in different outfits under bright lights or noon time sunshine. Make sure you're brightly lit. Analyze your footage to make better, more flattering wardrobe choices.

Summary
- Wear breathable, wrinkle resistant clothing made from wool, cotton blends, or rayon.
- Wear properly fitting clothing. Make sure there's no pulling at the buttons, tugging across the chest or clinging to bulges. You should be able to hug yourself without too much strain on the seams.
- Make sure your clothing properly covers your body.
- Wear clothing which is appropriate to your audience and message you're delivering.
- Choose clothes with colors that compliment your skin tone.

Clothing you should wear:
- Suits
- Great fitting tops, jackets, dresses and pants
- Solid colored clothing
- Professional uniforms.

Clothing to avoid:
- Clothing made of shiny, sheer or clingy material
- Slouchy, large gauge knit sweaters
- Turtleneck sweaters
- Patterned clothing with small, tightly clustered, high contrast stripes, dots or animal prints.

Chapter 4
Hair and Make-Up

Introduction

In all visual media, it's very important for you to bring your best face forward. You're presenting an image to an audience and you want it to be your best. Cosmetics and hair products are made to enhance your natural good looks. They make you more appealing to the viewing audience.

When making your make-up and hair choices, you should think of your face as a canvas and hair as its frame. Cosmetics and hair products are your paints and brushes. It's how you paint the canvas and frame the painting that distinguishes it as a work of art.

Hair

Hair is as individual as the wearer. My best advice is to wear a haircut that flatters your face and the shape of your head. Consult a professional hair stylist or barber to find the right hair style for you.

The only thing we directors ask is that you keep your hair off your face. Bright studio lights shine down upon your head. Harsh shadows from stray hair will mar your face with unflattering shadowy lines. Heavy chunks of hair hanging over your face will hide your eyes. The audience wants to see your eyes. Also fly-away hair or hair sticking up from static electricity can be distracting especially if you're working in front of a blue-screen. Tame your hair with hair spray, mousse, or gel.

In summary, consult a hair stylist for the best cut and products for you. Keep stray hair off of your face and out of your eyes and always check your hair in a mirror prior to going on air.

Make-Up

Television make-up has evolved with the technology itself. Instead of the heavy pancake make-up used in early films, today's make-up artists use air brushes to apply color and contour the face because HDTV's pictures are so sharp, almost every skin pore can be seen. Professional make-up artists with high tech tools and pigments are the reasons why movie stars look so good on-screen. But most television studios do not supply professional make-up services. You are responsible for your own make-up. You can hire a freelance make-up artist but they are expensive, charging on average $100 an hour. Or you can achieve television make-up with over the counter cosmetics. Theater actors, Las Vegas showgirls, and local news anchors apply their own make-up and so can you. But first you need a little free help.

Consult a professional make-up artist at your local cosmetics store or department store cosmetics counter. They'll give you good advice on which colors flatter your skin tone. They can demonstrate application of products on your face. If you can't afford the cosmetics they suggest, take their advice and find the same colors for less at your local drug or grocery store. Brands such as L-Oreal, Cover Girl, and Maybelline look just as good as their more expensive counterparts. Don't let the sales clerk sell you an entire line of skin and beauty products. You don't need lots of expensive make-up to look good on-screen.

Also, there are some great books, blogs and YouTube videos out there on make-up and its application. Remember, good make-up comes down to the right colors for you and how they're applied.

Everyday Cosmetics for TV

Because make-up color tends to wash out on television, you want to wear make-up that can stand up under bright lights. You want to use make-up which comes from a theatrical world with rich, vibrant saturated color. Brands from the modeling world such as MAC, Bobbi Brown, and NARS are excellent choices. The three make-up essentials you need are concealers, face powder, and lipstick.

Liquid Foundation and Concealers

No one's face is perfect. Most of us need a little help to conceal our imperfections; blemishes, acne, scars, or dark under-eye circles. You want a smooth, even skin tone on television. Foundation and face powders are ways to even out your skin tone. The amount of coverage you need depends on the condition of your skin or the number of flaws you need to cover. For heavy to moderate coverage, use liquid foundation with or without a concealer and set with a brush of loose face powder. For moderate coverage, use a concealer on blemishes followed by a dusting of loose or pressed face powder. For light coverage, use loose or pressed face powder. Here are some professional tips on how to match foundation and powder to your skin tone.

Choose liquid foundations where you can see the product in clear bottles. The color is truer than colors printed on packages. Pick a shade which matches the color of your skin *on your jaw line*. Your jaw line is a more accurate place to match color than smearing it on the back of your sun exposed hand.

Apply concealers with a concealer brush, blend out streaks and sharp edges then set with a brush of loose face powder. You can also apply concealers with a dry or semi-wet cosmetic sponge for a lighter application.

Loose and Pressed Face Powders

Use powder to dull unnecessary shine. Choose face powders where you can see the product through clear packages. Match the make-up to the skin on your jaw line. Apply a light dusting of powder to the face with a soft wide or round powder brush. You can apply pressed powder with the powder puff included in the compact case. Make sure to blend away excess powder.

Lipstick and Lip Gloss

Matte lipsticks or lipstick over a lip liner are recommended by make-up professionals. Unless you're going for a nude lip look, your lipstick should be saturated with color.

Many women love lip gloss but it should be kept to a minimum. Because studio lights reflect off lip gloss, it makes lips appear fuller but greasy. It is a good enhancer for women with thin lips. But for everyone else, a little lip gloss on the bottom lip looks better than an all-over application.

Avoid frosty lipsticks. They look cheap under bright lights.

Choose a lipstick with stay-on power. Faded or cracked lipstick will make you look old. Remember to moisturize and re-apply lipstick or lip gloss minutes before going on-air.

Eyes and Cheeks

Make-up for eyes and cheeks are as individual as the wearer. It depends on the look you're going for; natural, glamorous, sultry, edgy, etc. It depends on who you'll be addressing. More important, it depends on your facial shape and skin tone. So get professional advice to get the look you want.

You want to avoid unnecessary shine on the face. Make-up such as bronzers, and metallic or glittery eye shadows are meant to highlight your cheekbones, eyelids and under the brow. Unless you want to look like a Las Vegas showgirl, keep this make-up to a minimum.

Blush is a caution make-up. It's meant to accentuate the apple of your cheek, cheekbones and contour hollows. Some women tend to put on too much blush or blush which is too dark or too bright. You don't want to look like a clown. You want a healthy glow and/or more definition to your cheekbones. Blush is tricky because correct application depends upon the shape of your face. Get professional advice on the right color and application for you.

For Women

If you go to a department store cosmetics counter for a consultation or make-over, explain to the cosmetician that you need strong make-up which will be photographed under bright lights. Colors should be vibrant enough for the cameras to see. The make-up should be applied almost as heavy as the make-up you wear when going out at night but still look natural.

Just like your wardrobe, your make-up should be appropriate for the audience or show on which you're appearing. If you're speaking in front of a conservative audience, you may want to keep your make-up on the conservative side. It can be trendy for a teen show or natural for a morning talk show. Know your audience and play to their taste.

On the day of the shoot, you want to arrive at the studio as *camera ready* (in full wardrobe, make-up and hair) as possible. You may not have time or the proper facilities (i.e. a dressing room with a lit make-up mirror) to start from scratch so put on your usual day make-up at home. Remember to tame and shape your eyebrows. Apply all extensions (hair extensions, false eyelashes and acrylic nails) at home. Don't change your daily beauty regimen or try new products on your face the day of the shoot in case you have an allergic reaction to them.

Once you're at the shooting location and settled in, apply a little more eye shadow and/or blush, freshen your lips with lipstick, moisturizing balm, or lip gloss. Dust or blot away any shine on your face a few minutes before going on air.

For Men

Most men don't want to wear make-up but it can be beneficial to your overall appearance. You're on television to persuade people. Use everything in your arsenal to do so, including make-up. See Case Study #2 for an example of how make-up may have affected the outcome of a U.S. presidential election.

For most men, a light dusting of face powder on the face to dull the shine is sufficient. For bald or balding men, a dusting of loose face powder on the bald spot or scalp is recommended. Studio lights can leave shiny glare spots on bald heads. Eliminate glare with a light brush of matching loose face powder. Make sure your powder matches your skin tone and blends in. If you feel uncomfortable shopping in the cosmetics department, ask a female friend or relative for help. But remember, the professionals at department and drug stores won't bite so get their advice. If you don't want to use face powder, take a handkerchief with you to blot away perspiration and shine prior to going on-air or between segments.

Remember to groom your eyebrows, beard, or moustache. Get rid of noticeable nose and ear hair. Also, take lip balm with you to the studio to avoid cracked, chapped lips.

Case Study #2 - The Power of Make-Up

In 1960, United States presidential candidates Richard M. Nixon and John F. Kennedy participated in a series of debates in which the first ever televised presidential debate occurred. One televised debate, which was simultaneously broadcasted on radio, became the most decisive debate of the series.

Nixon was suffering from a cold. Though he was offered a make-up artist and advised to wear make-up for the TV cameras, Nixon refused. During the debate, Nixon stood hunched over the podium, looking pale and sweaty. Kennedy wore make-up as advised. He stood with good posture and gave an easy smile. According to polls taken after the debate, radio listeners felt Nixon had won the debate while television viewers thought the more photogenic Kennedy won the debate. Kennedy went on to win the Presidency.

Yeah, guys, your TV image can be that important. Your image is not only weighed in the court of public opinion, it can be measured in dollars and in Nixon's case, votes. If a little make-up helps you get what you want, you should consider wearing some to your next important on-screen appearance.

Summary
Wear what feels comfortable on you and is appropriate for the event. Remember, make-up is meant to accentuate your good features and minimize the flaws. Get a professional's advice on how to bring out your best features. Photograph yourself in different make-up and make adjustments.

Chapter 5
In the Studio

Introduction

Television stations are exciting albeit intimidating places. Bright studio lights, microphones, cameras and production staff scurrying around using unfamiliar broadcast language; it can be a stress filled environment that can overwhelm even the most experienced of speakers. But it doesn't have to be this way for you.

This chapter teaches you a bit about television production while preparing you for your studio visit. It'll show you how to prepare, what to take, what to expect, the roles of production staff, proper use of microphones, broadcast lingo, where to look when on-camera and so much more. By reading this chapter, you'll be less intimidated by the studio and more comfortable when working in front of cameras. The results; better performances and smoother media experiences for everyone involved.

Pre-Production Preparations

A well-run show uses pre-production check lists and rehearsals to achieve flawless shows. So should you. Your preparation is essential to your success so be prepared. I can't stress this enough. The worst presentations and interviews I've ever seen were given by people who weren't prepared.

First of all, be ready to answer the 5 W's of journalism: Who, What, Why, Where, and When. These are basic questions every journalist use.

Who - Who are you or your organization?

What - What do you do? What is your product?

Why - Why do you do what you do? Why is it special?

Where - Where can one buy the product? Where is the event?

When - Date, day of the week, and time of an event. Are there deadlines or expiration dates viewers need to know?

Confidence comes when you know everything about your subject matter. Be comfortable answering the 5 W's. You should be able to describe yourself, organization, or product in 50 words or less. Practice until you can answer them without thinking. Time yourself. You should be able to answer each of the 5 W's within 15 to 20 seconds because a typical segment in a television show is around four minutes long. Actors have scripts to memorize. Singers must know the lyrics to a song. You too must be prepared with what you want to say. You most likely won't have cue cards or a Teleprompter. You can't read a list of points from an index card while on-air or write them on your hand, so come prepared.

Also, as a part of your preparations, you should consider bringing a press kit.

Press Kit

A *press kit*, also called a media kit, is a packaged set of promotional materials of a person, company or organization. They're given to media outlets to announce a product release or distributed as information packets at news conferences. They often include:

- A press release detailing current developments
- A fact sheet listing specific features, benefits or statistics
- Media contact information (communications officer, spokesperson phone number, e-mail addresses, websites, etc.)
- A backgrounder - historical information
- Biographies of key executives, individuals, artists, etc.
- Photos or other images of key executives, logos, products, etc.
- Relevant DVD videos
- Past press coverage.

Your press kit doesn't have to include everything listed but you should take relevant material or samples with you to leave behind.

Pre-Production Dos and Don'ts

Do a dress rehearsal in front of a mirror at home. Put on potential wardrobe choices and practice your routine. Practice any demonstrations and their set-ups. Record yourself and review to make editorial changes as needed.

Use the Studio Check List on page 44 and create your own on page 73.

Be on time. Arrive at least a half hour before air time or as recommended by your studio contact.

Don't drink too much coffee or water thirty minutes prior to the shoot. Consuming too much liquid on top of nerves can make you want to use the bathroom. Once you're *mic'd up* (the technician has attached a microphone onto your shirt) it's too late for a last minute trip to the bathroom. Use the washroom when you arrive at the studio. It's a good idea to have a sip of water prior to going on-air to avoid a dry throat cough but don't chug the whole bottle. If you must use the bathroom after you've been mic'd up, make sure your microphone is off or on 'mute' before proceeding. Remember to turn it on when you're back on set.

Tell the production staff in advance of any electrical needs or special set ups. Some demonstrations require electricity, cables, tables, Wi-Fi passwords, or other set-ups. Large props, animals or special equipment may require larger access doors or set-up space. Tell your production contact at least 24 hours in advance of any special needs so they can accommodate your request.

You may want to bring an extra shirt and jacket. If you're shooting more than one episode of a show in one day, you want to bring additional clothing to change into. Also, an extra shirt is good in case the shirt you're wearing is problematic or you spill something on it. Bring them pressed and on hangers.

Production Staff

There are many people behind the scenes of a television show, both technical and non-technical. Listed on the following page are the people you're most likely to encounter on your studio visit.

Executive Producer - In charge of the program series. Manages budgets, coordinates with management, advertisers, financers, producers and talent.

Associate Producer - Assists producer, coordinates talent and pre-production schedules.

Field Producer - Assists producer or assumes producers' responsibilities on remote field productions.

Production Assistant - Assists the producer and director with production tasks.

Director - In charge of directing talent and technical operations during a live show.

Floor Manager - In charge of all activities on the set. Cues and directs talent and relays directors' orders. The floor manager will direct you on where to stand or sit and make you feel at ease.

Audio Technician - In charge of audio operations including microphone placement.

Engineer - Maintains technical equipment and troubleshoots problems during production.

Technical Director - Does the switching between shots and acts as technical crew chief.

Camera Operator - Operates the camera.

Be kind to everyone you meet, from the receptionist to owner. They are the gatekeepers of the media world. They're important to your on-air success. Listen to and respect the production staff. They are the experts who make you look good.

Studio Check List
Remember to take these items with you to your media appearances.

- Grooming aids - hair brush or comb, mirror, make-up, hair spray, lotion, antiperspirant
- Bottled water
- Cough drops and mints
- Tissues (Kleenex) or handkerchief
- Promotional materials: business cards, product samples, and leave behinds (coupons, order forms, brochures, web site address)
- Directions to the studio and parking
- Demonstration equipment, props, electrical cords, etc.
- Other. Make a list of any additional items you need to take with you on page 73 or store it on your phone or mobile device.

44

Pre-Interviews

Some times on sit-down interview shows, you may be asked to take part in a pre-interview. This is an interview with an associate producer who'll ask you some detailed questions about yourself. It may take place in a phone interview days before the show or happen upon your arrival. They may ask you the 5 W's or for an interesting or funny anecdote. The associate producer provides this information to the show's producer and host. Final questions are written on cards or tablets for the host to refer to during the show.

It is not a good idea to try to control the pre-interview. Restricting their topics and questions, giving them a list of the questions you'll answer, or demanding to know their questions in advance are counterproductive moves. You cannot control the outcome of any media interview, especially not this way. You'll only anger the show's producers who may take it out on you by asking even worse questions or never inviting you back to the show.

You may be asked questions you consider "off limits." If the questions are too personal, politely let them know. The only topics which are universally accepted as off limits are questions about your children or family. Everything else is typically fair game.

Don't ignore the producers' calls or be too busy for a pre-interview. Use it to your advantage. Remember, a pre-interview gives you some insight on what their line of questioning will be. You'll have an idea of what they're going to ask so you're not taken by surprise. It gives you a chance to press the points you find important and discourage questions you find objectionable. Be ready to answer difficult or personal questions. Remember to phrase all answers positively which leaves you in a positive light.

Working in Front of Cameras

Unless otherwise directed, use these broadcast industry standards to deliver a smoother, more professional performance.

On the Production Set

Your on-air success depends upon your professionalism. Be as professional as possible. Observe the rules of the set.

Turn off your cell phone. Cell phones use the same radio frequencies as wireless mics and may interfere with the audio. Even if your cell phone is on vibrate or silent mode, radio signals are still transmitting incoming texts, calls to voicemail, e-mail notifications, etc. to your cell phone. Turn OFF your cellphone.

Watch for cables on the floor while walking on the set. The set is a dangerous place. There are dimly lit areas, thick cables and sand bag weighted light stands on concrete floors. Be aware of cables on the floor and don't trip while walking

Don't touch any lights. There is both heat and electrical danger associated with studio lights. They heat up to extremely hot temperatures and can ignite flammable items (hair, clothing) or explode after contact with fingers so keep a good distance from lights.

Don't lean against any light stands or poles. Lights supported on stands are top heavy and can easily tip. Also stands with collapsible telescope rods may collapse and pinch your hand.

Be quiet on the set. Usually the floor manager will call out, 'quiet on the set' notifying cast and floor crew that they're about to go on-air. If you're waiting in the studio, either off the set or on, you must remain quiet when a program is taping or live on-air. Don't talk to others. Muffle all coughs and sneezes, and don't fumble with items only to drop them on the floor.

Live on air means you are LIVE ON AIR. There is no stopping, no re-takes. If you make a mistake, don't stop talking, yell 'cut' or ask if you can start again. This will ruin the show's continuity. There is no editing of live shows. Editing only happens on time delayed or recorded shows. Only the most egregious actions such as nudity, profanity, or unexpected violence are edited out. Everything else you say and do is going out to households and is recorded as such. If you slip up, shake it off and keep going.

Don't walk off the set in anger during the show. If you become angry at questions or actions lobbied against you during a show, don't storm off the set. It's unprofessional and can be dangerous; you can be blinded by lights, trip over cables or walk into a dark dead end behind the set. Keep your cool and let your host know what they said or did was inappropriate and explain why. Unless you are physically attacked or injured, finish the segment and talk to the producer about your concerns during the break or after the show.

Microphones
Microphones (*mics*) are sensitive, delicate, expensive sound amplification instruments. They should be treated as such but they are often the most abused piece of production equipment on the set.

You will most likely use one of two standard mics; a *dynamic mic* or a *condenser mic*. A dynamic mic is a handheld mic. It's rugged and can withstand high sound levels without overload damage. A condenser mic, the one clipped onto clothing or mounted to a podium, produces a higher quality sound which makes them very sensitive. They can easily become *over modulated* or so overloaded with sound that audio is distorted and undecipherable like a bad fast food drive-thru speaker.

Putting on a Lavaliere Microphone
A *lavaliere mic* is a clip-on wireless mic used by most television stations. In most instances, an audio technician or floor manager will place the mic on you. If you are handed the mic and asked to mic up yourself, you want to do the following. Thread the cable up underneath your shirt, blouse or jacket from the bottom up, so that the cable doesn't show on top of your shirt. Pinch the clip at the mic's head and attach the mic to the outer most clothing such as your tie, jacket lapel or blouse with the mic head pointing up. It should be approximately six inches below your chin. Clip the battery pack to your waistband above your hip. Make sure there's no hair, scarves or jewelry (chains, chunky necklaces) hitting or brushing against the mic's head. Make sure the mic head is pointing up.

You may need to readjust the mic during a sound check. Simply pinch the mic's clip and move it either up or down an inch, making sure nothing is rubbing against the mic's head.

Do not shove the battery pack into your pocket. Doing so can interfere with transmissions, causing audio to crackle or cut in and out, and damage the attached antenna which must hang unencumbered.

There is an on/off switch as well as a mute button on the mic's battery pack. The audio tech will make sure it's on. If you need to sneeze, cough or leave the set for privacy, you may want to mute your mic but you must remember to turn it back on.

Microphone Dos and Don'ts

Don't blow into the mic. People think blowing into the mic is an acceptable sound check. It is not. Over time, blowing into a mic will damage its working components. When asked to do a sound check, simply talk into the mic in your normal speaking voice.

Always speak into the mic. Audio is integral to television. Make sure you are heard.

Hold a hand held mic 3 to 6 inches from your mouth. Stay within one foot of a hand held at all times. If you are holding a hand held mic, do not drop it by your side or wave it around while talking.

If you are speaking into a mic mounted on a podium, there's no need to lean into it as they are sensitive condenser mics which are designed to pick up your voice at a further distance. Stand with good posture and project a strong voice.

Do not sneeze or cough into the mic. Muffle your sneeze or cough with your arm or hand or use the mute button. If you use the mute button remember to turn it back on. Use cough drops to quiet coughs and soothe a dry throat.

Do not throw or drop a mic. Please respect the equipment.

Don't hit the mic with your hands. Many times, people pat their chest to emphasize their passion. Don't pat your chest with a mic on. Don't cause unintentional noise by hitting the mic with your hand.

Don't clap into the mic. Clapping hands close to the mic can cause feedback.

Avoid causing feedback. *Feedback* is a disruptive sound of rings or ear splitting squeals resonating through an entire audio system. It is the worst problem for an audio technician to solve. Feedback is caused by a variety of actions; dropping a mic, holding two mics too close together, hearing aids, the sound system is too loud, a fist pounding a podium on which a mic is mounted, etc. Sometimes the only way to make the ring go away is to turn off the entire sound system then turn it back on. If you hear feedback, stop talking immediately and wait for a technician to fix the problem. Resume speaking once you're given the okay.

Always assume your mic is ON. Though you may think the microphone is off, production staff can hear everything you say in the control room. Don't say anything you wouldn't want everyone to hear. Your comments may be recorded or accidently go out on air.

Even when the floor manager gives the all clear after a segment, re-corders are still recording so remain silent.

Also, there is no such thing as "off the record." You can't rely on a reporter's promise that what you say in confidence won't go out on-air or leaked to the public. Don't let "off the record" comments sink your career. (Read Case Studies #3 and 4 later in this chapter.)

Do clip a lavaliere mic on the side in which direction you'll be speaking the most. Ideally, the mic head should be placed directly under your chin but if you'll be speaking to someone seated to your left, clip the mic onto the left lapel. If your audience is seated to the right of your center, then place the mic head on the right as you'll be looking their way as you speak.

Don't let a boom mic distract you. A *boom mic* is a mic held by a long pole hovering above the head or below the knees. Ignore it.

Do not remove the clip-on mic yourself. Wait for production staff to remove it or directs you to do so yourself.

Do not walk away with the mic. If you take off a mic by your-self, leave the mic on the chair in which you sat or on the nearest tabletop. Better yet, make sure it's left in the hands of the person who gave it to you.

Turn OFF your cellphone. Cellphones interfere with wireless microphones. If you must keep your cellphone on, leave it off the set and as far away as possible from the mics and microphone receiving equipment.

Speaking Into the Microphone
There are some physical adjustments you must make when using microphones. Keep these points in mind.

Always speak into the microphone. Depending on the type of microphone, one should always be six to twelve inches from your mouth, farther if you're singing loudly or shouting. If you're holding a hand held microphone, do not let the hand holding the mic drop down to your side and continue talking. We can't hear you.

Do not chew gum on air. Beyond the smacking sound going out on-air, it's rude and makes the chewer seem unsophisticated.

Don't rush your speech. Some people speak really fast when they're nervous. Slow your pace. Take your time. Take a deep breath and exhale. Practice the 5 W's at home.

Don't use profanity or foul language. If you curse regularly, break the habit because one will slip out at an inopportune moment.

Speak at your normal voice's volume. The audio technician will make amplification adjustments. Don't yell into the microphone. If asked to speak up, either speak a little louder or, if the mic is mounted, get closer to the mic and keep speaking.

Follow the interviewers' lead and don't interrupt. Let the host finish asking the questions before answering.

Follow the floor managers' leads and cues. You'll read about them later in the Floor Manager Cues section.

Don't look down and read from a script. You need to establish eye contact with your host, audience or camera. You can't read and maintain eye contact at the same time. Plus your bowed head will give us a lovely shot of the top of your head. Know what you want to say. Any notes should be in bullet point. Look up from your notes. The audience wants to see your eyes.

Remember to mention the key point you came to say. Always return to the main points you came to make.

Microphone Problems with Everyday Equipment
There are some everyday electronics which may interfere with microphones. Please be aware of them and the adjustments you may need to make to resolve any audio issues.

Black Berry Noise
As I've mentioned before, wireless microphones use radio frequencies to transmit audio signals to a receiver which in turn sends your amplified voice to the audience. Cellular phones use the same set of radio frequencies for phone calls, e-mails, texts, notifications, etc. Many cell phones use radio frequencies in a random fashion. Like the random action of a ball on a roulette wheel, the odds are low that your cell phone frequency will land on the same frequency as a wireless mic. A Black Berry phone signal is different. Its signal rotates regularly among radio frequencies and is guaranteed to hit your microphone's frequency at any given time. The result is an audible "fttt, fttt, fttt' or buzzing noise on air, in public audio (PA) systems and on recordings. The noise problem became so prevalent and annoying, audio techs in the broadcast world named it 'Black Berry Noise', after the offending device. It's a very distracting noise that

can ruin a good show.

To minimize the potential of Black Berry noise disruption make sure your cellular phone is turned all the way off. If you absolutely must keep your phone on, keep it as far away as possible from microphones and microphone receiving equipment.

Hearing Aids

A note about hearing aids. With an aging population, there are more people with hearing aids. Hearing aids can be a source of feedback. Because they amplify sound to the user's ear, that amplified sound can bleed into the user's microphone causing feedback. Some newer models are compatible with PA systems, but problems can still occur. If you wear a hearing aid to the set, advise the audio crew so they can make any adjustments on their audio board if needed.

If you are wearing a hearing aid and hear a squeal or ring through the speakers, simply turn down your hearing aid or back away from the mic. Between your effort and the sound crew's adjustments, the problem should clear up.

Field of View

When the camera operator *frames a shot* that means he's composing a picture with the camera. His job is to create a picture which conveys energy and is pleasing to the human eye. When framing the shot, he chooses his *field of view* which is how wide or close the shot is around the subject. This is important to you because if you want to be seen on the screen, you must remain in the field of view.

Again, the field of view depends on the camera operator or director. When a director tells the camera operator to zoom in or out, to save time, they typically call out shot designations of the *long shot* (LS), *medium shot* (MS), *close-up* (CU) and *extreme close-up* (ECU). The abbreviations are used in television and movie scripts. A long shot takes in a full shot of the subject from head to toe. A medium shot is a partial shot from mid torso to the top of the head. A close-up shot includes shoulders and face while an extreme close-up is a tightly framed shot around the face. For example, say you're making a video of a man standing in a state park talking about nature. The first shot is far away shot of the man in his entirety with the sky, mountains, river and trees behind him. The next shot may be closer to the man, shot from his waist up cutting out the sky and mountains. The next shot of the man is closer, shot from the chest up and the last shot would be a close-up shot of the subject's smiling face.

Staying in Frame

Again, it is essential that you remain in the field of view or *stay in frame*. You don't want to lean, bob or step out of the picture. It's important for you to adapt your performance to the dimensions of the camera's field of view. Your movements become exaggerated when on-air so it's important to pull them back. Keep these dos and don'ts in mind at your next media event.

Standing

Don't rock from side to side or shift from foot to foot. The field of view is narrow. A side step to the left or right can send you out of the shot. Plant your feet and stand still. Stand with confidence.

If standing in front of a podium, don't lean on it. Stand up straight.

Stand on the blocking mark as directed. A *blocking mark* is a mark (usually an 'x' made of tape) on the studio floor where talent is told to stand. These marks are made in advance for lighting and focusing reasons. It's important for you to *make your mark*, move to or stand where you're directed to stand.

Never turn your back to the camera. Unless it's part of your act or you're directed to do so, don't turn your back to the camera.

Sitting

Sit up straight. Don't slouch.

Don't swivel or rock in your chair. Plant your feet and keep them there.

Don't lean back then lean forward then lean back. The top of your head will bob in and out of frame.

Don't suddenly stand up. If you suddenly stand up, you will stand out of frame and we'll have a shot of your crotch until the camera operator adjusts the shot or they switch to another camera. Remain seated until told otherwise.

If you're wearing a suit jacket, sit on the back of your jacket. This keeps it from bunching around your shoulders and making you appear hunched over. Smooth your hands down your back and tuck it underneath as you sit down.

Where to Look When On Air

It may be confusing where to look when you are on-air. Do you look at the camera, the host or at the audience? It depends on the type of production. If you're being interviewed in a 2 person shot (you and the host) watch the host and follow the host's lead. If your host looks at you, return your gaze to the host. If the host looks into the active camera, you look into the same camera. The active or live camera's *tally light*, the red light above the camera lens, will be lit to indicate which camera is *hot* or active. Look into the camera only when the interviewer does. Do what the host does. If you're both seated and the host leans forward while speaking to you, then you lean forward. Follow your host's lead.

If you're speaking to an audience, look into the audience. Remember to look around at various spots in the audience like the back row, mid rows, and make eye contact with the important people in the front row.

If you're in a one person interview, where you're in a room by yourself such as a webcast, interview via satellite, or remote feed, you need to look directly into the camera lens. The camera is your audience. You must convey your energy into that lens to establish the contact you want. If looking into the lens scares you, focus your gaze at a point right beside the camera.

Many studios use robotic cameras. They move or swivel about the set without a cameraman present. If the camera starts moving, don't be alarmed. Don't look at it or pay it any attention. Continue talking to the host.

You will see monitors placed throughout the set. They are there for cast and crew reference. You may catch a glimpse of yourself on camera. Do not keep glancing at the monitors or become enamored with your image. Stay focused on the host, pay attention to the floor manager, and always know which camera is hot. Use the monitors for reference like a pro. If you notice that a part of your body, like your hands, are accidently in your host's one shot, move out of the shot.

Beating Camera Lens Nervousness

Looking into a camera lens scares a lot of people. They think of the thousands perhaps millions of people watching them. Don't let the camera lens scare you. The camera is simply what or who you want it to be. When you look at the camera, think about looking at your friends, your lover, or enemy; whatever works for you to establish the familiarity you want. You must not only look at the camera but look *through* it to connect with your audience. Again, if the lens scares you, find a reference point right above or beside the camera lens on which to focus your gaze.

Gestures and Body Language
People interpret your body language every day. From smiles and frowns to the way you stand or walk, everyone has an opinion about you based upon your body language. Most of this judgment is based on cultural and societal biases but either way, the public's perception of your body language can affect your desired outcome. Negative body language such as crossed arms, yawning, rolling eyes, exasperated sighs, an all-knowing smirk, throwing up hands in frustration or picking your nails can impact your outcome. A shocked look on your face is considered a *reaction shot* which can be used in any context.

The lesson to learn is this: **consider yourself on camera at all times**. Keep a pleasant poker face even when you think you're off camera. Don't be a robot without emotions, but keep your actions and reactions in check. Remain professional at all times. Demonstrate positive body language. A slight nod means you're listening and receptive. Folded hands say you're demonstrating patience. Unless negative behavior is your shtick, remain open and willing.

Keep your hand gestures to a minimum. They may fly out of frame or into another's shot. Keep them down, below your chest. If you fold your hands, don't wring your hands or twiddle your thumbs. It'll be interpreted as nervousness or boredom.

Good posture is important to your image. Stand or sit up straight. Don't lean on furniture (podium, table) or slouch. Bad posture may be interpreted as disrespectful.

Floor Manager Cues
The floor manager's job is to relay the directors' orders to the talent on set. Though many show hosts receive instructions through ear pieces linked to the control room, most stations still have floor managers that use a standard set of hand gestures or *cues*. Listed are the most commonly used hand signals and cues you're most likely to see.

Stand-by - the floor manager extends his hand up like a traffic cop signaling stop. The show is about to start. Get ready to be on-air.

Countdown - the floor manager will hold up ten fingers and count down on them with a verbal countdown to 2. The last 2 seconds are silently mouthed because the mics are now open or on.

Cue talent - the hand will swing down and point to talent. You are LIVE ON-AIR.

Most hand gestures relate to time concerns. The ones you are most likely to see are:

Speed it up - the floor manager points upward and rotates a hand in a circular motion. Whatever you're saying or doing, do it faster. There is little time left.

Slow down - the floor manager's hands pull away from each other in a stretching manner. There's more time left than anticipated. They want you to stretch it out so slow down what you're doing or talk some more.

Wrap it up - similar to the speed up gesture but the floor manager's hand is extended above his or her head as it rotates in a circular motion. Hurry up and finish what you're doing or cut to the finished product or final comment.

The most important cues you'll get are when you're about to go on-air and when approaching the end of the show. Respect the wrap up. You have 5 to 15 seconds to make your summary or finish what you're doing. Stop when the host says, "we have to go."

During the show, a floor manager may make gestures to indicate there's a problem with you or equipment. They may use hand signals to get you to speak up, readjust your mic or move over to the right. They may point to your glasses or watch, indicating they want you to take them off because they're causing glare. It can be like playing a game of charades. Use common sense while correcting the issue as inconspicuously as possible. Don't repeat their silently mouthed in-structions out loud.

When the interview or performance is finished, stay seated or standing where you are. Maintain a pleasant face and remain quiet until the floor manager indicates you're off the air, usually by saying, "And we're clear."

Remote Feeds and Compressed Image in a Box

All televised news shows employ an effect which compresses images into boxes. This effect allows multiple images to appear on-screen at the same time. It lets multiple people from different locations appear simultaneously on the screen. Typically included are the host, one or more guests and a montage of clips pertaining to subject. Because these boxes are small, close-up shots will be employed and you will be framed in a tight box. You have no wiggle room. If you suddenly sit up straight after being hunched over or lean one foot to the left or right, your face will bounce out of frame. So remember:

- Sit up straight and stay still (not too stiff.)
- Do not rock or swivel in your chair.
- Wait for your cues.
- Look straight into the camera.

One problem with remote links is satellite delay latency. A TV signal relayed over distance through multiple link-ups can result in a time delay of a few seconds. An example of this is when a news anchor in New York talks to a reporter in Cairo, Egypt and it takes a few seconds after the anchor stops speaking for the field reporter to respond. It takes that long for the anchor's signal to reach Cairo and vice versa. A host can wait up to 10 seconds for the questions to arrive to the interviewee. A time delay makes quick banter very difficult. Don't let this throw you. Wait for the host to finish speaking before answering and remain quiet until the next question. Don't interrupt the host or try to talk over other remote feed guests.

You may have an earpiece to hear your remote host or directions from the director. Hide the cord by tucking it behind your ear and clip it onto the back of your shirt's collar. Conceal it with hair if you can.

Some studio remote feeds use blue screen technology. Don't wear light blue or green if blue screen is being used. If you're unsure if blue screen is being used, ask your studio contact prior to the show.

Demonstrations

Demonstrations such as cooking a meal, showing jewelry on a home shopping show, or showcasing animals involves on-air talent maneuvering products. Typically the segment begins on a long or medium shot of the demonstration area, including you, the host and the product. Because the human eye tires of an image after three seconds, the director will choose a variety of shots to keep the viewer interested. Shots will vary from a LS of the entire set to an ECU of the product. For successful demonstrations, remember the following:

Be prepared and organized. Bring everything you need to the studio (use the Studio Checklist.)

Have your products or craft in various stages of preparation lined up in a row. You want to move smoothly down the line and not have to double back. If you're cooking or demonstrating a craft, have a completed craft or fully prepared meal ready to show at the end as you won't have enough time to finish the craft on-air. Your audience wants to see the payoff so have one ready.

Leave the product on the table for a close-up shot. When talking about it, don't snatch it up and move it around. The camera can't get a steady close-up of the item. If you see an ECU shot of the product on a monitor, don't fidget with it. Keep your fingers out of the shot and leave it alone for at least ten seconds as you continue talking about it.

Avoid glare on the product. Bright studio lights can leave glare spots on highly reflective items like plastic DVD cases and glossy book covers. If you see that happening, simply tilt the product down and away from overhead lights.

Group Performances

Bands, cheerleading squads, animal trainers or performers who perform in large spaces must adjust their set-ups or routines to fit into a tight studio space and field of view. Practice in tighter quarters and make adjustments to the act. When taking a group shot, stand very close together to get everyone in the shot.

For Models

For models, it's important to always be on time and look your best. Your job is to follow directions, smile, move about smoothly and put products in their best light. Like everyone else, you must be prepared.

Wear flesh colored undergarments that match your skin tone or black lingerie especially if you're modeling clothing. Your white bra under a black blouse or canary yellow panties under white pants could ruin the entire look.

Make sure you have nicely manicured nails and smooth hands for close-up shots. If your hands have noticeable veins or liver spots, you may want to apply sheer liquid foundation or a dusting of facial powder onto the back of your hands. Make sure it looks natural.

Remember to bring grooming essentials (make-up, lotion, hair brush, hairspray, etc.) Use the Studio Checklist.

When you pose or hold up merchandise, such as a ring on your finger, hold it still in place for at least five to ten seconds to allow the cameraman to focus upon you or the product.

Always smile and pay attention to direction. Gaze at the camera but pay attention to direction.

Fly Away Cameras

A *fly away camera* is a camera positioned above the stage on a track or guide wires and is run by robotic control. It's meant to get an omnipresent, 360 degree view of you. It was not intended for you to look directly into it. Unless told otherwise, do not look directly into this camera. Ignore it. Amateur talent mistakenly looks into this camera as it moves, twisting their head over their shoulder to maintain eye contact as the camera moves behind them. Doing this makes the talent look vain.

Case Study #3 - The Microphones are Never Off

The headline read "CNN Sorry for Reporter's Live Mic Incident."

CNN issued a public apology after anchorwoman, Kyra Phillips' off camera comments were accidently broadcast during a live speech by President George W. Bush.

On August 29, 2006, a conversation between Ms. Phillips and another woman was heard on-air as President Bushed marked the anniversary of Hurricane Katrina. Ms. Phillips microphone remained on while she was on break. Roughly 90 seconds of Ms. Phillips' conversation was broadcast over the President's speech.

As President Bush was on the screen, Ms. Phillips could be heard saying, "My brother is handsome and he is genuinely loving, you know, no ego…I've got to be protective of him. He's married, three kids and his wife is just a control freak." At this time, a voice (production staff) cuts in to tell Ms. Phillips to turn off her mic as her comments were being heard live on air.

CNN apologized to the public and the White House saying,

"CNN experienced audio difficulties during the president's speech today in New Orleans."

Case Study #4 - There's No Such Thing as "Off the Record"
Veteran journalist Connie Chung's interview techniques were gentler than her contemporaries but in 1995, Chung faced a career ending controversy. In an interview with Kathleen Gingrich, mother of Speaker of the House, Newt Gingrich on the TV show *Eye to Eye*, Mrs. Gingrich stated she couldn't say what her son thought about then first Lady Hillary Clinton on the air. Chung asked Mrs. Gingrich to "just whisper it to me, just between you and me," knowing full well the microphones would catch her comment. Mrs. Gingrich leaned in and the whole world heard her say, "He thinks she's a bitch."

Like most people, Mrs. Gingrich interpreted Chung's suggestion of whispering the statement into Chung's ear was a promise that the statement would be off the record. It wasn't. The stunt ultimately backfired on Chung. When the program aired, viewers felt Chung had compromised her journalistic integrity by tricking an old woman with no media savvy into making an embarrassing and divisive statement. It's been suggested that CBS, looking to drop Chung from her contract, made no defense of the incident and released Chung from her contract.

Summary
In summary, when you're on set, be professional, courteous, and ready to perform. Be mindful of mics, don't say anything you wouldn't want broadcast to the entire world and follow all cues.

Chapter 6
Handling Negative Media and Public Scrutiny

Becoming a Public Figure

One becomes a public figure, intentionally or by circumstance, when one becomes a public curiosity. When you put yourself into the public realm such as performing on television, posting pictures on Instagram or running for elected office, you can become a public figure. You can also become a public figure if you're associated with an unfortunate event such as being a victim in a sensational crime or involved in a scandalous affair. Just being linked to a person of notoriety either by relation or association can make you a public figure. It's unfair but true.

One downside to being a public figure is loss of privacy. People may point at you as you walk down the street, hound you for a statement, ask you for a selfie while you're eating in a restaurant or camp outside your home with cameras. You may feel that this is a violation of your privacy and that once you become a public figure, you lose some of your rights to privacy. In some ways that's true but privacy issues are complicated. For example, if you make your own sex video and it's released to the public without your consent, you won't win an invasion of privacy case because you gave away your privacy once you recorded it. But it's private, meant for your eyes only, right? Although it was not intended for the public to see, many courts have determined that when you record yourself, you trade away your expectation of privacy. This is just one of the many issues relating to a person's right to privacy versus the media's rights to pursue a story.

Public figures attract not only media, but fans and critics alike. You will have your supporters but no matter what you do, you will be criticized. Putting yourself out there means you must shake off negativity. It's a hard thing to do but when you're exposed to public scrutiny, you can't let peoples' negative opinions affect you.

We live in a media driven culture. You should know your rights as well as the media's rights. You should know how to deal with intrusive, unwanted or negative press.

Managing Intrusive Press

The media is double edged sword. It keeps us informed of current events and can be used to get our message out to the masses. But sometimes, in the pursuit of a story, media outlets can become aggressive. It's nothing personal. That's how they pay the bills.

There are some definite dos and don'ts when dealing with aggressive or intrusive press.

What to Do if Ambushed by the Press

An *ambush* is when a number of uninvited reporters descend upon you asking explicit answers during difficult times. Ambushes happen in public places (sidewalks, parking lots) for two reasons; because the subject is being reclusive and the only time to catch them is in public and two, there's urgency to the story. The press has a right to approach you on the sidewalk or any other public space such as courthouse steps. The American constitution guarantees Freedom of Speech and Freedom of the Press. That gives media outlets the constitutional right to pursue a story unencumbered. That doesn't mean they can do whatever they want. They can't follow you onto private property i.e. a house, restaurant, office building or your front yard, without the owner's permission. If they do, they are trespassing and you have a right to demand them to leave.

So you're coming out of your house and a reporter sticks a mic in your face or you're getting out of your car in a parking lot and you're surrounded by a hoard of cameramen. What do you do?

Keep walking when approached by unexpected press. Don't stop to talk. Keep moving to your final destination. If there's a large number of reporters or they become too aggressive for you to walk safely, turn around and go back from whence you came. It you're in a building, try leaving from another door.

If you're at home and they keep knocking at your door, you may answer the door or ignore them altogether. If you do open the door, crack it open. Do not make any statements. Tell them you have no statements at this time, politely ask them to leave your property, and shut the door. They must return to the sidewalk. You can't ask them to move any further back than the sidewalk because the sidewalk is public property and they have the constitutional right to be there. You may call your neighborhood security or the police for assistance if they refuse to leave your property or become disruptive to the neighborhood.

Designate a spokesperson. You can hire a public relations firm or lawyer, or assign an articulate relative to be your spokesperson to the media outlets. They should have a statement to read on your behalf.

Never touch a photographer or his camera. If you try to block the camera lens with your hand or touch a camera man, you are breaking a federal law. You are interfering with that photographer's constitutional rights (Freedom of Press.) Depending on the nature of the assault (shoving, spitting, punching, damaging equipment) the photographer can bring assault and battery charges against you or sue civilly for damages. Remember, no matter how much they crowd or annoy you don't let your emotions get the best of you. Keep your hands off the photographer.

Do not let the press provoke you into negative comments or actions. No matter how stupid or insensitive their questions may be, don't let your emotions overcome you. Some disreputable press or photographers may shout hurtful comments to incite negative reactions. Don't let them bait you into a confrontation. Just walk away.

Do not answer questions with "no comment." This is a stale cliché. The best thing would be to say nothing. If you must address the press, you can say, "I'm not prepared to answer that question at this time," or "I'll have to get back to you on that," and then do so. If you're with your family or on your own time, you can say, "I understand you have deadlines but please respect my privacy. I have nothing to say right now."

Don't publicly criticize the media's coverage of you. If you live by the media, you can die by the media and they do hold grudges. Criticizing a news organization can hurt you in the future. The next time you deal with the press, they may play tough by throwing hard-ball questions at your press event. They may refuse to cover your events or product launches. They may even hound you harder. If you develop a problem with a certain news outlet or reporter, or you believe you've been libeled or slandered, you or your lawyer should speak directly to the news managers, producers, sales reps (if you bought commercial time on that channel) or station owner for an acceptable resolution.

Handling Negative Press

The best way to handle negative or unwanted press is to ignore it altogether until it goes away. This is a very hard thing to do. Most people can't. They let their emotions control their reactions which can give the media more to talk about. If you absolutely can't stay quiet, here are some ways to manage unwanted media.

Reiterate your message. No matter what the question is, just keep repeating the points you want to make. Give the media representative a press kit or written statement from which they can glean the facts they want for their story. If the media keeps coming to your house, you may want to leave some statements outside your front door for them to take away.

Don't get caught up in watching news or blogosphere coverage of you. Public relations nightmares are made when clients watch too much of their own press coverage. They over react and insist upon contacting the press because they need to 'get the story straight.' This can make matters worse. Be aware of the coverage about you but don't be obsessed about it and let your emotions lead you into saying or doing something stupid. Just back away from it, keep your emotions in check, and take breaks from media coverage including your social media accounts.

Take action if media statements made about you are blatantly untrue. If libelous or slanderous statements are made about you, you should contact the media source for a public correction, retraction, or apology. If the media outlet continues to make untrue statements or there's no resolution to your complaint, you can hire a lawyer and bring a civil suit against them. But remember, you must prove that the statements are untrue, malicious and damaged your reputation or business to win (See Libel and Slander on page 65.)

Don't be a nuisance to a media outlet. If you want to correct misinformation a news organization may've reported about you, you may call and speak to the reporter who reported it. But do not keep calling them. Do not flood their office with e-mails or faxes. You will accomplish nothing and will put them off to do anything for you in the future.

If you or your company caused a negative situation, never say you're sorry. Though you may feel sorry, apologizing indicates you know what you did was wrong and implies that you're responsible for the results. Instead of apologizing, say, "It's unfortunate that the situation has occurred."

Use other media, such as social media, your website, or newspapers to post your position in a positive light.

Do not lash out on your social media. Do not post angry statements, e-mail responses or post videos when you're emotionally charged or you will make things worse. Before posting any video, watch it ten times sober. Before posting a statement, wait until the next morning and read it again. You might change your mind.

Legal Issues with Media

You have the right to privacy, that's true. But the media has rights too. Sometimes individual rights collide with the media's rights when it comes to freedom of the press. Where do you stand as far as dealing with unfair press? This is by no means legal advice. These are statements of fact based on court rulings regarding legal issues between individuals and the media.

Freedom of the Press

In America, the media enjoys certain freedoms guaranteed in the U.S. Constitution; the First Amendment rights to Freedom of Speech and Freedom of the Press. They have the right to express opinion, ideas, and information without interference. If you interfere with their rights of expression, such as blocking the camera with your hand or snatching a camera from a photographer, you are violating their right to freedom of speech.

Libel and Slander

Most complaints against unfair press include claims of slander and libel. Slander and libel are both part and parcel of defamation; a false claim, either stated or implied, to be factual in which an individual, business, product or groups' reputation is harmed. The difference between slander and libel is that slander is a harmful statement made in a transitory form such as speech or spoken word. Libel is a harmful statement in a fixed medium like newspapers, leaflets, signs and in durable form such as CD's, DVD's, websites, blogs, and film.

Most states allow a person to take legal actions, civil and/or criminal, against those accused of libel and slander. People who think they can win a libel case must understand that suing media outlets and individuals for slander and libel is an expensive, high risk proposition that rarely pays off. Statements made as "facts" are actionable. Statements referring to that of an "opinion" or when one says "allegedly" before making the statement are not actionable. A slandered individual must prove that the statements were presented as fact, that they were false, malicious, and were expressly meant to hurt the plaintiff's character or business. Most can't prove slander or libel and lose. In order to win damages in a libel case, the plaintiff must show that the statements made by the media are "statements of fact or mixed statements of opinion and fact" and that these statements are false. If the statements are so ridiculous and untrue, such as your mother is a donkey, then you won't win your case because no one would believe such an outrageous allegation. Very few people win slander and libel cases.

Waivers

A waiver is a release form. It is a legal document which gives the production company permission to use your likeness in any way they like. You are, in essence, signing away your rights to control your image and/or voice in relation to the show. You are permitting the company to use your image and/or voice on-air, in promotions, commercials, or in American Idol's case, for comic relief.

On-air talent waivers that come from reputable news stations and media outlets are standard and typically fair to talent, but you should always read it. It is a contract in which you are signing away some rights. Question anything that doesn't seem right. If you don't feel good about it, get legal advice before signing. But remember, if you don't sign it, you more than likely won't be on the show.

A waiver is not a waiver of liability which means you are not signing away your rights to sue if you are injured on the show. You're only signing away control of your image and voice pertaining to that show.

The Dark Side of Media Exposure
Cyber bullying

Most media outlets offer internet on-line content. On-line stories and videos often have comment sections for readers or viewers to leave their comments. It's meant to stimulate social interaction and provide feedback for the media outlet monitoring community reaction to the story or content. Some people post positive comments but for the large part, the comments section often attracts negative remarks from hateful people. Don't read the comment sections. There are some very mean spirited people out there who have nothing better to do all day but write offensive remarks. Avoid them altogether.

If someone keeps commenting on you on your social media page, don't engage your antagonist with a response. Upsetting you makes them feel better. If you do engage, it will escalate and you will not win. You may even make things worse. Don't reply to their remarks. Block them from your account, pity them and move on. If a person maneuvers around your block and the comments become excessive, you can report the situation to the website's webmaster. The web-master can take down the comments, close the offender's account and ban the person from making further comments on the site. The last option is for you to close your account, remove your video, and stay off the internet for a while.

If the cyber bullying escalates or results in criminal actions like stalking, vandalism or assault, report it to the police and take legal actions against that person or group. Otherwise all comments are considered free speech and there's not much more you can do about it.

Stalkers

You may encounter a stalker; a person who is obsessed with you. These people can be scary and dangerous. If you receive numerous or threatening e-mails, unwanted phone calls or items, or visits from an obsessed person, document them and report them to your local police. Do not talk to these people or accept any of their gifts. Let the police and courts speak for you. You can get a restraining order against the person and in some states stalkers can be arrested or held on a 72 hour psychiatric evaluation.

Become more observant about your surroundings. Don't get paranoid but be aware of the people in your surroundings and follow your intuition. In extreme cases, you may have to change your phone number, stay off the internet or even move. Please take obsessed fans and all threats seriously.

Paparazzi

I can write an entire book on the paparazzi and the court orders, legal issues, and legislation they've generated around the world but I'll keep it brief. You probably won't encounter them in your lifetime but just in case.

Paparazzi are independent contractors who sell their photographs or videos of celebrities to media outlets. They typically run in packs and wait for celebrities to emerge from public places like restaurants and airports. They're aggressiveness has been well documented over the years. They've caused car accidents and run into celebrities with bikes on the sidewalk. They've followed and harassed celebrities dropping off their children at school. One rented a room in a house beside an actress' home in the Hollywood Hills and photographed her from his upstairs bedroom whenever she was in her bathroom. They've taken photographs of a topless duchess on a castle terrace from nearly a mile away. There's almost nothing they won't do or place they won't go to get the shot.

The paparazzi have incited some celebrities into violent encounters. Celebrities have lashed out by yelling at, pushing or hitting photographers, and smashing or taking their camera equipment. Of course these incidents are all caught on other paparazzi cameras and used against the celebrity in court. Celebrities have been fined, have settled financially out of court, and have even been jailed for physical attacks on the paparazzi. And though it seems the paparazzi have all the power, their aggressive actions have generated legislation and ordinances all over the world. For example, California Senate Bill SB 606 increases penalties for the intentional harassment of children of famous parents as defined by their profession.

Though the paparazzi are a nuisance, they are protected by First Amendment rights. The best way to fight them is with civil action. They are still subject to criminal penalties associated with trespassing, stalking, voyeurism, reckless driving, computer hacking and harassment. In recent anti-paparazzi laws, the media outlets are fined thousands of dollars if they use illegally gotten photographs. This dissuades media outlets from buying photographs from disreputable photographers. What is an illegally gotten photograph? In the case of the photographer who rented a room to photograph an actress in her bathroom; using a telephoto lens to peek into her bathroom from dozens of yards away produced illegally gotten photographs because being in her bathroom entitled the actress to a reasonable amount of privacy which he violated with his voyeurism.

If you are the subject of paparazzi, treat them like ambush reporters. Keep moving. Don't react to their questions. If they're being polite and the questions are light, you can talk to them or pose for a picture. Sometimes once they get the picture they want, they'll leave you alone for a while (as they upload photos to their buyers.) If they continuously follow you for weeks, you can file for an injunction or restraining order against them. If they follow you in a car, don't try to outrun them. There have been many accidents caused by paparazzi chasing their subject and like Princess Diana, it can lead to death. If they surround your car on foot, please be careful as you slowly maneuver away. Don't let the paparazzi incite you into doing something stupid.

Surviving Scandal

The best way to survive scandal is to keep a low profile (limit events, avoid parties, stay home) and wait for an even bigger scandal to happen and knock you off the front pages. They always do.

It's hard to stay out of the spot light once it's been focused on you. Depending on the nature of the scandal, media coverage can last for days, weeks, or even months. It's nothing personal. Scandals are reality shows which we all know makes for good TV. They go through three stages: the flare up, the simmer, and the cool down. It starts with the media's pack mentality and public curiosity. They become more intrusive, knocking on your door, following you to your car. The reporters' questions become more personal as they try to provoke a response from you; anger, laughter, tears. It simmers when the scandal is played over and over again on news outlets and dissected by experts and analysts. And ultimately, it will cool down then quiet as the next bit story piques the public's interest. As time drags on, the public tires of it, and it becomes a distant memory. A scandal is destructive. It disrupts your business, your home and family and disturbs society's consciousness. It's emotionally and physically draining. Do everything you can to prevent a scandal because once it starts, all you can do is ride it out like small boat in a bad storm.

Endnote

I've given you a lot of information to digest. But if you read every page and took the advice to heart, you'll give much better performances than before. You've been given the secrets of successful celebrities and on-air personalities so keep this guide with you for quick and easy reference before on-air appearances. Remember, people want to see you succeed so be the best you can be.

Studio Checklist

_____Grooming aids - hair brush or comb, mirror, make-up, hair spray, lotion, antiperspirant

_____Bottled water, cough drops and mints

_____Tissues (Kleenex) or handkerchief

_____Promotional materials: business cards, product samples, and leave behinds (press kits, order forms, menus, etc.)

_____Directions to the studio and parking

_____Demonstration equipment, props, electrical cords, rechargers, etc.

Other:

_____

_____

_____

_____

_____

_____

www.ingramcontent.com/pod-product-compliance
Lightning Source LLC
Chambersburg PA
CBHW021212020426
42331CB00003B/326